The 40

A Forty Day Devotional to Finding Peace, Purpose, and Passion

The 40

A Forty Day Devotional to Finding
Peace, Purpose, and Passion

Todd Boffo

© 2024 by Todd Boffo
The 40
A Forty Day Devotional to Finding Peace, Purpose, and Passion

All rights reserved solely by the author. The author guarantees all contents are original and do not infringe upon the legal rights of any other person or work. No part of this book may be reproduced in any form without the permission of the author. The views expressed in this book are not necessarily those of the publisher.

Scriptures marked ESV are taken from the THE HOLY BIBLE, ENGLISH STANDARD VERSION (ESV): Scriptures taken from THE HOLY BIBLE, ENGLISH STANDARD VERSION ® Copyright© 2001 by Crossway, a publishing ministry of Good News Publishers. Used by permission.
Scriptures marked NIV are taken from the NEW INTERNATIONAL VERSION (NIV): Scripture taken from THE HOLY BIBLE, NEW INTERNATIONAL VERSION ®. Copyright© 1973, 1978, 1984, 2011 by Biblica, Inc.TM. Used by permission of Zondervan
Scriptures marked NLT are taken from the HOLY BIBLE, NEW LIVING TRANSLATION (NLT): Scriptures taken from the HOLY BIBLE, NEW LIVING TRANSLATION, Copyright© 1996, 2004, 2007 by Tyndale House Foundation. Used by permission of Tyndale House Publishers, Inc., Carol Stream, Illinois 60188. All rights reserved. Used by permission.

Printed in the United States of America.

ISBN-13:
979-8-9910780-09 Paperback
979-8-9910780-16 Hardcover

Double Helix Publishing
Fountain Hills, Arizona

DOUBLE HELIX
PUBLISHING

TABLE OF CONTENTS

INTRODUCTION VII
DAY 1: CHASING GREATNESS 1
DAY 2: GOD IS BIGGER THAN THE STORM. 5
DAY 3: INVITE GOD INTO YOUR DAILY DECISIONS 9
DAY 4: DON'T LET FEAR HOLD YOU BACK 13
DAY 5: HE GIVES POWER TO THE WEAK. 17
DAY 6: USE YOUR GOD-GIVEN GIFTS 21
DAY 7: SHOW GOD'S LOVE 25
DAY 8: STAYING SHARP, SCALING YOUR SUCCESS 29
DAY 9: CONTROL YOUR ANGER 31
DAY 10: DON'T SETTLE FOR MEDIOCRITY 35
DAY 11: YOU ARE SERVING THE LORD 39
DAY 12: A CHANCE AND A CHOICE 43
DAY 13: MAKE AN IMPACT 47
DAY 14: YOU ARE CAPABLE 51
DAY 15: FORGIVE OTHERS 55
DAY 16: BE CONTENT 59
DAY 17: HE CARES FOR YOU 63
DAY 18: BE STILL, FIND YOUR INNER PEACE . . . 67
DAY 19: THE PEACE OF GOD 71
DAY 20: PRAY FOR WISDOM 75
DAY 21: ALL FOR GOOD 79
DAY 22: DO NOT FEAR 83
DAY 23: THE LORD IS MY HELPER. 87
DAY 24: GOD KNOWS BEST. 91
DAY 25: FINDING ULTIMATE FULFILLMENT 95

DAY 26: AN EVER-PRESENT HELP 99
DAY 27: LIVE PEACEABLY 103
DAY 28: GOD BLESSES A GENEROUS SPIRIT ... 107
DAY 29: STEP OUT IN FAITH 111
DAY 30: ALL FOR GOD'S GLORY 115
DAY 31: SEEK AND OBEY.................... 119
DAY 32: REJOICE ALWAYS................... 123
DAY 33: SPEAK LIFE INTO OTHERS 125
DAY 34: HE STRENGTHENS US 129
DAY 35: THE STRENGTH OF MY HEART....... 133
DAY 36: SEEK THE KINGDOM 137
DAY 37: ESTABLISH MY STEPS 141
DAY 38: SERVE GOD, NOT MONEY........... 145
DAY 39: LOVE GOD AND LOVE OTHERS....... 149
DAY 40: RICH IN REPUTATION 153

NOTES 157

INTRODUCTION

You are a world changer. You live and work in the real world, grinding it out every day. You are creative, resourceful, and know how to get things done. People depend on you. Whether you are a C-Suite Executive, Entrepreneur, Manager, Independent Contractor, or Consultant, these daily insights were pulled together just for you.

You are busy. You don't have the luxury of a long morning devotional before your day spins up into productivity, problem solving, and crushing it. But maybe you would like to spend just a few minutes with your mind on God. Maybe you know you need Him in your life, and you want to be more proactive in your relationship with Him.

I've had the privilege of working with and building friendships with industry leaders and entrepreneurs like you from across the globe. I have learned we all have the same struggles, doubts, and hardships, no matter our occupation or net worth. I've gained some valuable insights along the way, and for the next forty days, I want to give you some daily encouragement and help you recalibrate your life with God more clearly in the picture.

If you can spare five minutes, I would love to share a bit of truth for a better life.

DAY 1:

CHASING GREATNESS

"Now the Lord said to Abram, 'Go from your country and your kindred and your father's house to the land that I will show you. And I will make of you a great nation, and I will bless you and make your name great so that you will be a blessing. I will bless those who bless you, and him who dishonors you I will curse, and in you, all the families of the earth shall be blessed.'"

Genesis 12:1-3, ESV

Feeling stuck in a rut, unsure of how to break free and pursue the dreams inside you? That could be a sign you are called to something greater. Just like God called Abraham to leave his comfort zone and embark on a new journey, you might also be on the verge of a significant change in your life. Whether starting a new business, chasing a career opportunity, or making personal life alterations, growth requires change. You can't expect your life to change for the better if you never take action.

But change can be daunting. It's natural to feel anxious about taking risks. Knowing God has a plan for your work and personal growth can make all the difference. By placing your faith in His guidance, you'll find the courage to embrace change and become the person you're meant to be.

If you feel unsteady about embracing change, I encourage you to nurture your faith. Believe in the dream God has planted within you. You have a unique purpose in life, and by cooperating with God's plan, you'll not only grow, but you'll also become a blessing to others—just like Abraham. With God's help, there's no limit to what you can achieve.

Scan here for today's video

"Greatness is not in where we stand, but in what direction we are moving. We must sail sometimes with the wind and sometimes against it, but sail we must, and not drift, nor lie at anchor."

– Oliver Wendell Holmes Sr.

DAY 2:

GOD IS BIGGER THAN THE STORM

"Immediately, Jesus made the disciples
get into the boat and go before
Him to the other side while He dismissed the crowds.
And after He had dismissed the
crowds, He went up on the mountain
by Himself to pray.
When evening came,
He was there alone,
but the boat by this time
was a long way
from the land, beaten by
the waves, for the
wind was against them.
And in the fourth watch of the night,
He came to them, walking on the sea.
But when the disciples saw him
walking on
the sea, they were terrified, and said,
'It is a ghost!' and they cried out in fear.
But immediately, Jesus
spoke to them, saying,
'Take heart; it is I. Do not be afraid.'

Peter answered Him, 'Lord if it is
You, command
me to come to You on the water.'
He said, 'Come.' So Peter
got out of the boat
and walked on the water and
came to Jesus."

Matthew 14:22-33, ESV

Leaders are some of the loneliest people I've ever met, and the weight of this loneliness can be overwhelming. Being a leader means trailblazing in areas others haven't been before, and this will take you through storms, and you will find yourself in situations where you wish you had someone to turn to. As Jesus' disciples battled against the rising waves and the threatening winds, they probably felt this same way. While they fought for their lives on the sea, they thought Jesus was a long way off on the mountain, oblivious to what they were going through. Then, to their surprise, Jesus approached them on the water, taking charge of the raging storm and revealing He was at their side even when they least expected He would be.

Whether you're leading your organization through rough times, guiding your family through a crisis, or fighting on your own to make ends meet, you're never alone. God promises He will never leave or forsake us, but it's easy to get distracted by the waves.

Day 2

Sometimes the weight of our problems seems so great that we can't see a way through them. The good news is, we don't have to.

Jesus' disciples were terrified by the storm they were in, and to an extent, they had every right to be. Their situation was too great for them to handle on their own, but Jesus' presence changed everything. He saw them through that difficult experience, and as their relationship with Him grew, He enabled them to do amazing things to glorify God. The same is true for you.

God set you up to overcome, to achieve, and to build something important. Today take your eyes off the storm and see the God who calms the storm. See the God who will keep you from drowning. Whatever you focus on gets bigger, so make sure you see God as bigger than any storm you face. Just like Jesus calmed the storm and walked on water to rescue His disciples, He is always with you. He will help you in the middle of your storms. The secret is His presence. If you're in a storm right now, you're not alone.

Scan here for today's video

"God gives you a vision bigger than your pain threshold so you learn to have greater faith, greater hope and greater trust in what HE can do. Don't fight it because it's the process for becoming more mature."

– Todd Boffo

DAY 3:

INVITE GOD INTO YOUR DAILY DECISIONS

"Trust in the Lord with all your heart, and do not lean on your own understanding. In all your ways acknowledge Him, and He will make straight your paths."

Proverbs 3:5-6, ESV

Are you in the middle of making an important decision? One of the defining characteristics of a great leader is the ability to be decisive. Being able to make and execute a decision is a valuable skill, but I want to give a warning to all you high-level achievers. As you juggle family, finances, relationships, your career, and other affairs, you're not going to have all the answers you need to be successful.

Sometimes you are going to make a mistake.

You were created with the ability to reason, but this doesn't mean you'll never make bad choices. The fact is, we all make mistakes all the time. No wonder we were given verses like the one we just read! This passage in Proverbs is one of the first scriptures I ever memorized as a kid, and I write this scripture often when I sign my name.

The Hebrew word for acknowledge used in these verses is *"yada,"* which means to know, to perceive, to consider, or to be aware of. When we acknowledge God in all our ways, it means we recognize and respond to God's sovereignty and wisdom in our lives. It is understanding and accepting God as the one who guides and directs our paths. We must lean on Him and acknowledge Him in all our ways. God's not going to force Himself into your business. However, God shows up every time He's invited. God doesn't ever ask for your advice. He says, "I know the way and can show you the way!" Take time today to think about what areas you need God's wisdom. What paths are you on that need to be straightened?

Scan here for today's video

"Leadership is a journey guided by divine wisdom. Inviting God into our decisions opens the door to purposeful and impactful choices."

– John C. Maxwell

DAY 4:

DON'T LET FEAR HOLD YOU BACK

*"Have I not commanded you?
Be strong and courageous.
Do not be frightened,
and do not be dismayed,
for the Lord your God is with
you wherever you go."*

Joshua 1:9, ESV

No one guaranteed you an easy life. Even when you know your work aligns with God's will for your life, the difficulties you encounter can be pretty discouraging. When Joshua faced taking over leading Israel after Moses' passing, he knew he was following God's instructions. Even knowing it was God's plan, Joshua still needed some encouragement to move forward.

God told Joshua not to be afraid—to stand strong and have courage. Okay, great, but how? How could Joshua be sure he was leading the people in the right way, and what about the numerous enemies set against Israel? Fortunately, God never stopped telling him to have courage. He reminded Joshua that He would be there with Him to guide and strengthen His people everywhere they went, so the children of Israel had no need to worry. They could stand strong and be confident in the power of God. His hand was on them.

His hand is on you, too.

When I moved to Arizona it was one of the lowest moments of my life. My daughter had gone through a traumatic experience that would require intense therapy, relocation and prayers. Everything I had planned for my business, career and life was upended within a year of this devastating revelation. But God knew … He knew where we needed to be regardless of what it looked like. He still had a plan. And while I was worried, He had already worked it out. Trusting God's plan is not a theory for me— I am a practitioner!

Nothing great is ever accomplished without courage. Courage is an essential ingredient for building a life beyond what you've lived so far. Joshua needed encouragement because his actions would lead a generation into the Promised Land. "Be strong and courageous." Let these words also encourage you when faced with great or overwhelming tasks. Face your fears and take a step toward doing what

Day 4

God has called you to. He is with you every step of the way.

There are many people around you whose lives will be impacted and influenced because of your courage. Trust in God's presence and guidance; don't let fear hold you back from navigating life changes or pursuing your goals and fulfilling your potential.

Scan here for today's video

"Courage is found when I make the reason to do it greater than the reason not too."

– Todd Boffo

DAY 5:

HE GIVES POWER TO THE WEAK

*"He gives strength to the weary
and increases the power of
the weak.
Even youths grow tired and
weary, and young men stumble
and fall;
but those who hope in the Lord
will renew their strength.
They will soar on wings like
eagles; they will run and not
grow weary,
they will walk and not be faint."*

Isaiah 40:29-31, NIV

No matter how talented you are at what you do, you can probably relate to feeling weakness at some point. As you navigate your life, you'll find that the daily grind of work, relationships, bills and general life can sometimes be taxing.

I remember launching our company while moving into a new church building and navigating issues with my family. I was so overwhelmed I ended up in the ER with chest pains in my late 20's. But the answer to my problem was the man in the mirror. I had to change my mindset and how I viewed this season of my life. I chose a direction based on this principle: where God guides, He provides. When I learned to put more trust in Him than in myself it served me well!

You will get tired. Even the strongest among us grow weary. However, God calls us to hope in Him to renew our strength. At our lowest points in life, that's when God shows Himself most powerfully.

When you are at your weakest moments, hope in God! He is willing and able to renew your strength. God knows our true home is in heaven, and we will struggle here on earth. The good news is that He will renew our strength and increase our power until we can run our race without growing weary or faint. He will help us fight the good fight of the faith.

Scan here for today's video

"For my weaknesses are a portal
for God's power."

– Todd Boffo

DAY 6:

USE YOUR GOD-GIVEN GIFTS

*"For we are his workman-
ship, created in Christ Jesus for
good works,
which God prepared beforehand,
that we should walk in them."*

Ephesians 2:10, ESV

Have you ever felt like you've lost sight of your purpose? Many of us experience times when we question if we're on the right path. Perhaps you've doubted whether you chose the correct career, or maybe you've been certain about the industry you want to enter but uncertain about which specific role suits you best.

Sometimes it's hard to decide where you should be in life, especially if you have many different abilities and interests. In Ephesians, Paul shares that God has great plans for us and has given each of us specific gifts and abilities. In whatever you do, it's important to use your gifts to glorify God.

What gifts has God given you? If you aren't sure, take some time to think about it. If you don't know, ask Him—He'll answer.

I am currently working on my second book that is called *PRINTS: Unlocking the Secret of Why You Were Made For More.* It's based off the uniqueness of your God-given design. I created a course that will help uncover exactly how God designed you and get you closer to operating in your zone of genius and fulfillment.

God created you with a specific plan and purpose for your life—and that plan includes your work. You will spend a third of your life at work building your business or career, and God has built you to do it well! You're uniquely created with God-given gifts. Knowing what they are will give you an edge because every ability you have was entrusted to you with potential for growth beyond what you can imagine. It came from God, uniquely designed just for you!

Scan here for today's video

"Let every man abide in the calling wherein he is called and his work will be as sacred as the work of the ministry. It is not what a man does that determines whether his work is sacred or secular, it is why he does it."

– A.W. Tozer

DAY 7:

SHOW GOD'S LOVE

"Be completely humble and gentle; be patient, bearing with one another in love."

Ephesians 4:2, NIV

Getting caught up in competition and striving after personal success is easy to do. Achieving great things at work is commendable, but it's essential to remember the people around you. Today's verse encourages us to treat others with humility, gentleness, and patience.

Whenever the Bible mentions an action there's a reason and that usually means we won't want to do this naturally. We need God's help to exemplify these characteristics. It takes strength to be humble and incredible strength to keep unity, but that is the benchmark.

A mistake that makes you humble is better than an achievement that makes you arrogant. Who you will become is based on the decisions you make today.

Work can become so task-focused that people can get overlooked, but it shouldn't be that way. Not only is treating others with kindness something we are commanded to do in scripture, but it also creates a great working environment where people are productive and flourish. When the people around you feel respected and appreciated, respect and appreciation are reciprocated.

Remembering the value of humility, gentleness, and patience in our relationships with others is important. By showing love and grace toward our colleagues and co-workers, we can foster a positive and collaborative work environment and model Christ's love to those around us.

Scan here for today's video

"Talent is God given. Be humble.
Fame is man-given. Be grateful.
Conceit is self-given. Be careful."

– John Wooden

DAY 8:

STAYING SHARP, SCALING YOUR SUCCESS

*"If the axe is dull and
its edge unsharpened,
more strength is needed,
but skill will bring success."*

Ecclesiastes 10:10, NIV

As a kid, the winters in New Jersey meant some seriously cold weather, and my dad would have me cut, stack, and organize the wood pile at some point in October. Having a sharpened axe makes all the difference in the world when you're chopping for hours! If an axe is dull, it takes a lot more effort to chop wood, and there's a possibility of getting hurt if the dull blade skips off the log as you're swinging.

Are you encountering resistance in your life? Do things seem harder than they should be?

All leaders encounter times when they don't see the full reward for their efforts. There will be days when you work long hours on difficult tasks, and you won't always see immediate success. You will encounter obstacles and undesirable conditions, so how do you reach your accomplishments?

Scripture tells us that with skill, one can still succeed, even if the axe is not in perfect condition. There are seasons when you lose your edge, but you're not alone. This happens to everyone! Instead of focusing on the progress you think you should be making based on what others have done, run your race at the right pace. An unsustainable pace kills more people than distance ever will. Lean on your skills and push through resistance as you get your edge back—sharpen your axe—remembering that staying sharp is about being intentional and honest with where you are and where you want to be.

Scan here for today's video

DAY 9:

CONTROL YOUR ANGER

*"People with understanding
control their anger;
a hot temper shows great
foolishness."*

Proverbs 14:29, NLT

We all have emotions and for good reason. That passion and determination allow you to do what you do so well. But like any other skill, your emotions need to be honed. With the highs and lows you go through, it's natural to experience a wide range of feelings—from joy and relief to disappointment and even anger. There are many passages in scripture about that last emotion—anger—and it's clear that God knows just how destructive anger can become when unchecked.

If you let anger take control, there will be a cost. Being led by anger nearly always ends with getting you into trouble. Anger can fuel misunderstanding and cloud your judgment and your communication, causing division and leaving you more prone to making mistakes. When you lose your temper, you always lose. You might lose someone's respect, the love of your family, your health, your clients, or even your job. You can be right and still end up being wrong.

Ready for the good news? If you live empowered by the Holy Spirit, He will help you exercise self-control in any situation. Self-control is a fruit of life in the Spirit. Feeling anger is not the problem. Anger is normal. The issue arises when our response to our feelings causes us to be controlled by our emotions rather than us controlling them. Here's a tip that helps me: You don't have to attend every argument you're invited to! Disconnecting from others' disputes is extremely beneficial, and in a culture fueled by outrage and unrest, disconnecting is self-preservation! Life as a leader is difficult, and there are enough things that will frustrate you. There's no need to take on more mentally and emotionally taxing issues than necessary. No one is perfect, but with the blessings you are given come responsibility. Self-control is critical to sustaining greatness!

Scan here for today's video

Anger is an acid that can do more harm to the vessel in which it is stored than to anything on which it is poured.

– Mark Twain

DAY 10:

DON'T SETTLE FOR MEDIOCRITY

*"Do you see a man
skillful in his work?
He will stand before kings;
he will not stand before
obscure men."*

Proverbs 22:29, ESV

You worked hard to get to the place you are now. Success at any level takes perseverance and grit; you'll likely be exhausted after achieving something difficult. Doing things with excellence isn't always easy, and it can be a lot simpler to be satisfied with just getting by.

When things are good, it might be tempting to enjoy the current situation, but complacency will hinder you from the greatness you could achieve. Appreciating all you have accomplished is okay, but getting comfortable will hold you back. Solomon encouraged us that our work doesn't go unseen—skilled work results in opportunities—so it's important to keep growing and improving.

Strive for excellence in all that you do. A lifestyle of excellence is rewarded with open doors to lead and serve in a place of influence. Be grateful for the success you have achieved but don't get complacent. God sets the ceiling for your influence and you owe it to Him and the purpose on your life to keep growing. Aim to be skillful and excellent in your work and your relationships. Never stop developing your skills or bettering yourself. God wants us to be great!

Scan here for today's video

"Lord, help me to be seen so that I can become invisible. I want them to see YOU."

– Todd Boffo

DAY 11:

YOU ARE SERVING THE LORD

"Whatever you do, work heartily, as for the Lord and not for men, knowing that from the Lord you will receive the inheritance as your reward. You are serving the Lord Christ."

Colossians 3:23-24, ESV

It can be easy to think of certain aspects of your work as menial tasks. It's normal to have responsibilities you don't enjoy. Whether that's paperwork, cleaning, or something else rudimentary, we do these things because we have to, but have you ever considered that *how* you do these things matters?

When someone else—someone you respect—observes what you do, you probably feel motivated to work well, no matter the task. But how do you do these things when no one is watching? Our motivation shouldn't come from trying to gain approval from other people. Focusing on being a people-pleaser can create issues because others can develop unrealistic expectations of you—in essence, you train people how to treat you. While it isn't wrong to please others with our work, we were created with the bigger purpose of pleasing God. I'll never forget my grandfather telling me his thoughts about his experience growing up through the Great Depression, being a first generation immigrant from Italy. He said everyday we had to produce something, care for the farm animals before/after school, work hard at school and football so he could get a scholarship, etc. When you realize God has given you an opportunity, give it all you've got and the rewards will be great!

Remember that your work is not just for the benefit of your clients or your own personal gain; it is ultimately an act of service to God. Work with dedication and excellence, knowing that you are serving the Lord and that He will reward you for your faithfulness. In the same way, remember that every aspect of your life, not just work, is an act of service to God. I'm not saying He is a taskmaster that you must please; service to God flows from a grateful heart. It isn't a chore or a behavior box to check off. It is a natural response when your love for Him overflows. When that happens, you will serve Him with dedication and excellence. An added bonus is that God is faithful to reward you for your faithfulness to Him.

Scan here for today's video

"Work becomes worship when you dedicate it to God and perform it with an awareness of His presence."

– Rick Warren

DAY 12:

A CHANCE AND A CHOICE

"For it will be like a man going on a journey, who called his servants and entrusted to them his property. To one he gave five talents, to another two, to another one, to each according to his ability. Then he went away. He who had received the five talents went at once and traded with them, and he made five talents more.
So also he who had the two talents made two talents more. But he who had received the one talent went and dug in the ground and hid his master's money.

Matthew 25:14-18, ESV

Every day when we wake up, we have a chance and a choice. How will we use what has been given to us? Will we use it to grow and improve?

Or will we stay stagnant, so risk-averse that we bury our gifts in fear of what may happen?

Doing nothing with your gifts is safe. However, without taking risks, we also won't reap much reward. Taking appropriate risks is part of being faithful with what we have. In Matthew, Jesus told a story of servants who were given talents—a unit of money worth around twenty years' work for a laborer. Today, this equates to about $1 million. The ones given two and five talents each found ways to multiply what they were given. But the servant who got one talent was afraid of a loss from investment, so he buried the talent to keep it safe.

What a great lesson about how we should handle, grow, and multiply what is given to us—not just money but gifts, abilities, opportunities, and connections as well. Don't forget there's an expectation for us to grow everything God has given us. We all have different talents that will reap benefits only if we don't bury them. Don't be afraid to take risks and invest in yourself! Your destiny demands that you step out of your comfort zone and use your talents to the fullest.

Scan here for today's video

"You can't put a limit on anything. The more you dream, the farther you get."

– Michael Phelps

DAY 13:

MAKE AN IMPACT

*"Do not be slothful in zeal,
be fervent in spirit, serve
the Lord."*

Romans 12:11, ESV

Do you feel tired or worn out? The fact is, life is exhausting. Between work, family, and your own personal development, it's easy to feel spread thin. Considering this, you may think you have reason to take it easy occasionally, but this mentality mustn't give way to laziness.

You will undoubtedly be tired and experience wanting to throw in the towel, so how do you combat those feelings? Today's verse encourages us to be zealous and fervent—enthusiastic and passionate—when it comes to serving God. Stay excited and dedicated, knowing you glorify God in whatever you do.

When you start losing your zeal you have to get back to you WHY. The driving reason for which you were put here, at this time, with these gifts and for what mission. Don't let complacency or laziness hold you back from working hard. One of the ways you serve God is through your work. When you use the gifts He gave you to produce something, it pleases Him! You don't have to be a pastor or missionary—whatever work you do, when done for His glory as you live out a life of promise, functioning according to the design of your Creator, your work pleases God. Real estate, shipping, retail, consulting, banking ... it doesn't matter what you do; it matters who you do it for. Be passionate and enthusiastic about using your skills and abilities to serve Him. This will positively impact your career. I promise this is true.

Scan here for today's video

"We should be about more than just selling chicken: we should be a part of our customers' lives and the communities in which we serve."

– Truett Cathy
-Founder - Chik Fil A

DAY 14:

YOU ARE CAPABLE

*"I can do all things through
Him who strengthens me."*

Philippians 4:13, ESV

How often have you felt you had to do the impossible? Maybe you've been faced with meeting difficult deadlines, starting a business, or getting your family through a rough time. Wherever you are in life, whether you're just starting out on your own or considering the pathway to something new, you're probably familiar with feeling as if a goal you have is impossible to reach.

You might have a challenge before you right now that feels impossible to overcome, but today's verse, "I can do **all things** through Him who strengthens me," reminds you that you don't have to do things on your own. The things that are impossible for you are more than possible for God. You have probably heard this so often it sounds like a cliché, and even if you acknowledge this in your head, do you truly invite God into every aspect of your life? We need to welcome Him into our daily lives, especially in dire situations.

With God's strength and guidance, you are capable of achieving anything He has called you to accomplish. Don't let your limitations or setbacks hold you back. Trust in His power and ability to work through you. He will always equip you with everything you need to achieve what He's called you to do.

Scan here for today's video

"Turn down the volume on my own self-doubt and rejection and turn up the volume on my intuition."

– Jamie Kern Lima

DAY 15:

FORGIVE OTHERS

"Bear with each other and forgive one another if any of you has a grievance against someone. Forgive as the Lord forgave you."

Colossians 3:13, NIV

If you've worked long enough, you know how competitive business can be. As corporations compete for audiences and co-workers fight over positions, conflicts are bound to arise. It's part of it. But scripture cautions us against holding on to grievances or offenses. These turn toxic fast.

Division often takes root where unforgiveness flourishes, which does more damage than we may realize. When we hold onto grudges, we give place to the schism that hurts the people around us. The more time we spend in discord, the less effective we are at reflecting the love of God. In business I have been blessed with the best and worst of people. It can be heartbreaking when someone steals money, doesn't honor the contract or makes it impossible for us to work together. We still have a choice and we can't live as a victim, we must forgive and move on. You don't have the luxury of wasting any of your time, energy or emotions on people who are part of your past and not your future. It was a lesson learned and now it's time to move forward.

It's important to remember the value of forgiveness and grace in our relationships with others. If you struggle, remember all that Christ has forgiven you, and it gets a little easier to walk it out. By bearing with and forgiving one another, you will maintain healthy and positive relationships and model Christ's love and forgiveness to those around you.

Scan here for today's video

"Resentment is like drinking poison and then hoping it will kill your enemies. Forgiveness liberates the soul, it removes fear. That's why it's such a powerful weapon."

– Nelson Mandela

DAY 16:

BE CONTENT

*"But godliness with
contentment is great gain.
For we brought
nothing into the world,
and we can take nothing out of it.
But if we have food and clothing,
we will be content with that."*

1 Timothy 6:6-8, NIV

Have you been caught up in the pursuit of success and material possessions? It's easy to do as ambitious individuals, but it's important to remember that true contentment and fulfillment come from a relationship with God.

There is an internal struggle with every high performer to find the balance between being content and knowing we have been built by God to achieve more. We can help keep this in check by remembering it's fine for me to have stuff but stuff can't have me. You were built to grow and prosper based on your abilities and God's grace. There is a desperate need for kingdom minded, highly successful men and women who understand their marketplace ministry.

When you constantly look for other things to satisfy you, you'll discover that nothing will make you truly happy. Today's scripture reminds us that we came into the world with nothing, and we should be content with what we have, even if we think it isn't much. Discontentment leads to greed, and there is a better option for living than being driven by a never-ending desire for more.

Instead of just looking to stack up more accomplishments or gain more wealth, remember to obtain and clothe yourself with godliness. By focusing on what truly matters and being content with what you have, you can find joy and purpose in your work and personal life. Be thankful to God for everything you have—this is the secret to great contentment.

Scan here for today's video

"Contentment is enjoying what you have right now. If you don't learn contentment, you'll never be happy. You'll always want more."

– Rick Warren

DAY 17:

HE CARES FOR YOU

*"Humble yourselves, therefore,
under the mighty hand of God
so that at the proper time
He may exalt you,
casting all your anxieties on Him,
because He cares for you."*

1 Peter 5:6-7, ESV

Everyone likes to feel good about themselves, but hardly anyone enjoys spending time with a proud person. Have you ever wondered why that is? In many cases, a proud person takes the credit for their success, using their circumstances to exalt themselves. As followers of Christ, we can appreciate the goodness we have seen in our lives while attributing it to God, not ourselves.

Another aspect of pride is that it can keep you from trusting others. It takes humility to expose your weaknesses, including shortcomings and anxieties. Peter instructs us to humble ourselves under God, letting Him exalt us as we cast our cares on Him. You can trust Him.

Humility can be the greatest virtue while pride can be the greatest vice. It doesn't matter how much money, status or power you have at your disposal. Life and problems do not respect your status, life happens to everyone. In over 30 years of working with people at all levels, I have seen this lesson: we will humble ourselves or be humbled. Building a successful career filled with achievements isn't the problem. It's keeping the main the the main thing, all that I have and ever hope to be, I owe it all to Him.

God knows life can give us many reasons to be anxious. It's been said over 25% of people deal with anxiety. I remember my dad telling me, "Todd, 80% of what you're worried about will never happen. The only one who knows the future is God, so keep your focus on Him."

We all tend to either overestimate or underestimate our abilities depending on the situation. The word to "cast" here actually means to throw. It's the same Greek word used in Luke 19:35 when people threw their clothes on the donkey Jesus rode into Jerusalem on Palm Sunday. What a perfect example of how we are supposed to deal with our cares by giving them over to the Lord. He has set up a process for us to deal with life and the struggles we all face.

Day 17

Trust in God's timing and plan for your life. Cast all your anxieties on Him, knowing that He cares for you. The biggest burden in your life never takes God by surprise. It is never a struggle for God. While you're trying to figure it out, God's already worked it out!

Scan here for today's video

"True prayer is a way of life, not just for use in cases of emergency. Make it a habit, and when the need arises you will be in practice."

– Billy Graham

DAY 18:

BE STILL, FIND YOUR INNER PEACE

*"Be still, and know that I am God;
I will be exalted among
the nations,
I will be exalted in the earth."*

Psalm 46:10, NIV

In the fast-paced world of business, it can be easy to get caught up in the hustle and bustle and feel overwhelmed. Despite the distractions, it's important to take a step back and remember that God is in control.

If we fail to remember God's reverence, we fail to remember our purpose as individuals. While our work seems important, we were first made to glorify Him. He comes before everything else in our lives. In today's verse, "Be still" is a nice way of saying STOP—PAUSE. God is going to do something only He could do.

When I was younger, growing up in New Jersey, I worked in an Italian butcher shop. It was like living in a reality TV show with all the personalities and their stories that could be their own book! But I remember how the atmosphere would shift when someone from Angelo Bruno's family (a Philly mob boss) would come in. He would come in with two guys; they parked in front of the store, were always respectful, and never demanding. However, there was an obvious presence they carried that made everyone stop. People knew that if they told you something would be taken care of, there was absolutely no doubt or worry that it would be done. In the same way, God's presence should be welcomed and respected in our everyday lives. Sometimes the best way to fight is to be still and know that God's got you!

Remember to take time out of your day to be still—to stop and remember God. By finding stillness and quieting our minds, we can tune out the distractions and remember that God is sovereign over all things. Trusting in His power and goodness can bring peace and perspective in the midst of life's challenges.

Scan here for today's video

"I've never made football my priority. My priorities are my faith and my dependence on God."

– Bobby Bowden

DAY 19:

THE PEACE OF GOD

*"Do not be anxious about anything, but in every situation, by prayer and petition, with thanksgiving, present your requests to God.
And the peace of God, which transcends all understanding, will guard your hearts and your minds in Christ Jesus."*

Philippians 4:6-7, NIV

It's natural to feel anxious at times, especially when facing difficult challenges or uncertain circumstances. While momentary feelings of anxiety are normal, worry is something dangerous to hold on to. Because whatever you focus on grows larger, worry comes when you focus on the situations that trouble you instead of focusing on the One who can help.

Worry is when you create more problems and pain through your imagination then reality. The more time we spend worrying, the less time we spend recognizing and focusing on the greatness of God. Glorifying our issues over God is never a good idea. This is why God tells us through His Word to give up our anxieties and present our requests to Him.

This is how we combat anxiety. When we approach God with thanksgiving and tell Him what we need—what we're worried about—He promises to give us His peace, which surpasses all understanding and guards our hearts and minds. How great is that! God's peace can give us strength and perspective as we navigate the ups and downs of work and life. Tell God what things are on your mind today, and let Him comfort you with His unexplainable peace.

Scan here for today's video

"I pray to the Almighty to encourage you to dedicate your life to Jesus Christ. Whatever difficulties you may have to face, turn to him, recognize Him and render him all your glory, and he will help you overcome."

– Colonel Sanders

DAY 20:

PRAY FOR WISDOM

*"If any of you lacks wisdom,
let him ask God,
who gives generously to all
without reproach,
and it will be given him."*

James 1:5, ESV

You probably know the feeling of being unsure about what to do. There are so many uncertainties in life, which makes decision-making that much harder. As a corporate example, say you choose to hire an employee. You can study that person and use common sense to make loose predictions on what your hiring choice will cause, but you can't really know for sure how they will work out. So how do you know you're doing the right thing?

Even when you have really good judgment based on years of experience—relying on your own judgment can only get you so far. We have limited perspectives, and it's easy to miss important factors involved in decision making.

Wisdom closes that gap. Wisdom—seeing things from God's vantage point—is an invaluable attribute you need when making any kind of big decision. Consulting others with more experience, such as teachers or mentors, can expand your perspective, and they can weigh in with valuable advice, but perfect wisdom comes only from God.

Always turn to God for wisdom and guidance when facing difficult decisions or challenges. He generously provides wisdom to those who ask, and His guidance will lead you to success and fulfillment. I never walk into a business meeting or coaching session without asking God to help me understand the situation, show me what I need to see, and respond in a way that glorifies Him. It doesn't need to be a long prayer. Asking for wisdom is as simple as talking to God and inviting Him into life's situations. Godly wisdom is the key to accomplishing the God-sized purpose for your life!

Scan here for today's video

"My favorite business book is the Bible. If you study the Bible with a view to extracting principles on how to set up, and manage a business effectively, you will be absolutely amazed; it has everything."

– Strive Masiyiwa
Econet

DAY 21:

ALL FOR GOOD

"And we know that in all things God works for the good of those who love Him, who have been called according to His purpose."

Romans 8:28, NIV

Challenges and setbacks are a natural part of life. Although we expect them, it can be pretty discouraging when things don't go according to plan. We tend to have an ideal picture in our heads of how we think things need to happen for everything to work out, but often, God has other plans.

When our schedules go off track from what we originally designed, it's easy to get frazzled. You might be worried about whether things will work out, but Paul told us we don't need to be concerned. For those who love God and go about His work, God works everything out for good. You qualify for this benefit!

When you are walking a purpose filled life there are two parts, what you can do and what only God can do. When you've come to that place where you don't know the right answer, the right direction or have the right resources. This is the divine intersection of God's grace and provision. God loves you and has a purpose on your life so take care of his business and he'll take care of yours!

Even when things don't go your way, you can take comfort in knowing that God is working behind the scenes, using even the difficult or frustrating circumstances for our good and His glory. When you trust in God and seek to align your life with His purpose, you will find hope and purpose in any situation!

Scan here for today's video

"The Bible tells us that God always finishes what he starts. If you feel incomplete or unfinished, you can trust that God will carry on his good work in you."

– Rick Warren

DAY 22:

DO NOT FEAR

*"So do not fear, for I am with you;
do not be dismayed,
for I am your God.
I will strengthen you and
help you;
I will uphold you with My righteous right hand."*

Isaiah 41:10, NIV

What is something you currently dread? It might be bad news, concern about not getting something accomplished on time; it might be an uncomfortable conversation you need to have or anything else that causes you anxiety. We have talked about fear a few times already, but that is because fear is a common emotion, and how we handle fear impacts the quality of our life and leadership.

Whatever fears exist in your life it eventually becomes a boundary. Some boundaries are healthy and good for you. However, there's a calling on your life that goes beyond where you are today and to a place you've never been. Whenever you get to a place in life you've never been you will have two options, faith or fear. We all go down this same road but you have been built to grow and achieve more than you realize so stick with faith because fear is not your friend!

Numerous Bible verses speak on the subject, including the one we shared today. He will strengthen, help, and uphold you with His hand, so you do not need to be afraid of anything.

While God doesn't promise easy times, He does promise to be with us through every difficulty. We can take comfort in the promise that God will stand by our side, willing to strengthen and guide us. If you're feeling afraid, pray and invite God into your concerns, relying on Him to encourage you. He knows the struggle you're in right now, and you're not alone. When you trust in Him and lean on His strength, you can overcome any challenge. You will have peace and courage every day.

Scan here for today's video

"You must be very persistent, and you have to have the confidence in yourself that you can achieve that which you are seeking to accomplish."

– Cathy Hughes

DAY 23:

THE LORD IS MY HELPER

"Keep your lives free from the LOVE of money and be content with what you have, because God has said, 'Never will I leave you; never will I forsake you.' So we say with confidence, 'The Lord is my helper; I will not be afraid. What can mere mortals do to me?'"

Hebrews 13:5-6, NIV

What do you rely on when you find yourself in a bind? Is it your position? Your friends? Your wealth? Here's a hint: These things can't save you, and money is the *last* thing you should put your trust in.

There is nothing wrong with building a wealth in every area of life and we have a responsibility to use our talents to their fullest! But, the Bible warns us about the love of money and how it can separate us from God. Those who focus on money and possessions never find true happiness and peace. Money is a resource but should never be the driving source of our desire. True joy and security come from satisfaction and contentment in God.

Today's passage tells us to free ourselves from the love of money, embrace contentedness in God, and have confidence in the Lord. Money can bring many benefits but there are things money cannot buy and problems only God can solve . When you stumble into trouble, rely on God and trust in Him alone. With His power on your side, you don't have to fear anything man or the future can throw at you.

Scan here for today's video

"You don't have to understand everything; you just have to believe that God is protecting you."

– TD Jakes

DAY 24:

GOD KNOWS BEST

"A person may have many ideas concerning God's plan for his life, but only the designs of God's purpose will succeed in the end. The counsel of the Lord shall stand."

Proverbs 19:21, TPT

The more success we have, the more we grow confident in our abilities. The more competent we are, the more difficult it is to rely on God. I mean, if you are using the gifts God gave you, and you have been a great steward of those gifts and developed them into finely honed skills that serve you well, that's a good thing, right? Of course, it is. In fact, your excellence and achievements can bring God great joy. Don't you love it when your children apply themselves, do their best, and have great things to show for it?

Today's scripture reminds us to make sure we stick to and trust God's plan. I talk about this a lot more in my book *PRINTS: Unlocking The Secret For Why You Were Made For More*. I have a specific course designed to helping you clarify and construct this next season of your life in alignment with your unique design.

While we are busy building our lives, we don't want to skip consulting the Architect's blueprints. After all, God knew you before you were in your mother's womb. He crafted your personality, your preferences, your natural talents and spiritual gifts, and He chose where you would be born, to what time in history your life would be lived out, who you would live in proximity to, what problems you are uniquely wired to solve, and everything about you that makes you feel alive and free. Why wouldn't you check in with Him to make sure your plans are not going to cause you trouble?

All your goals and dreams are awesome—as long as you submit them to God and make sure they align with His plans for you. All of God's plans are good. All of His designs succeed. Next time you are alone and quiet, spend some time asking God what He has for you. You'll be glad you did.

Scan here for today's video

"When you trust God to write your story, it will be a story worth telling."

– Todd Boffo

DAY 25:

FINDING ULTIMATE FULFILLMENT

"Delight yourself in the Lord, and he will give you the desires of your heart."

Psalm 37:4, NKJV

We all have certain desires and goals for our careers and personal lives. Maybe you want to make enough money to create opportunities for your children or retire at a certain age, or maybe it's more important to you to improve society with your business. While we can have many good goals and desires, these will not bring us ultimate fulfillment. However much you achieve, you'll want more.

Sometimes we can get so caught up in chasing after **things** we forget that achieving our earthly aspirations will never satisfy us. Although our goals may be good, pursuing these desires is the wrong approach to fulfillment.

God isn't always giving us all the information or the complete picture. We need to have dreams, visions and action plans to see them come to life. But be open in that entire process and pray this prayer, its one of the most dangerous prayers you could ever pray. Not my will, but your will be done. Because we always have a limited view of the situation or circumstances and God has a funny way of weaving his plan into the one we have going on. When are closest to Gods heart when we love what God loves.

The Bible promises that if we delight ourselves in God **first**, He will satisfy us with everything we need—"all these things" are added as we seek Him first.

You will find joy and fulfillment in seeking God and delighting in Him. When you make Him the center of your life and seek to align your desires with His will, you can trust that He will give you the desires of your heart in the ways that bring Him glory.

Scan here for today's video

"When you delight in God, you find delight in life itself, for He is the source of all good things."

– Todd Boffo

DAY 26:

AN EVER-PRESENT HELP

*"God is our refuge and strength,
an ever-present help in trouble."*

Psalm 46:1, NIV

You know from experience that everyone will face uncertainties and challenges. It's guaranteed. When that happens, it's helpful to have friends and family to turn to in tough times. While having others around you in meaningful community is healthy, there's nothing like being able to turn to God for strength and protection.

The word refuge here means a shelter or covering from rain, a storm, any type of danger and a falsehood. God's umbrella policy of protection is all encompassing and provides divine protection because God knew we would need it. He's not far off watching things unfold, he is present with us in the struggle. Sometimes he calms the storm and sometimes he calms the child in the storm.

Because we live in a fallen world, life isn't without hardship, and trying to navigate difficulties on our own is exhausting. We need to rely on God for help as we go about our daily affairs, and we need Him even more when things aren't going well.

When we stumble into times of trouble, we can find hope and strength in the knowledge that God is our refuge and our ever-present, always-available, incredibly-capable help. In the midst of trying times and uncertain circumstances, you can depend on and rest in His constancy, strength, and love.

Scan here for today's video

"I put everything in God's hands. He's my strength, and without Him, I wouldn't be able to do what I do."

– Chris Weidman

DAY 27:

LIVE PEACEABLY

"If possible, as far as it depends on you, live at peace with everyone ... If your enemy is hungry, feed him; if he is thirsty, give him something to drink. In doing this, you will heap coals of fire on his head."

Romans 12:18, 20 NIV

You spend a lot of time at your workplace interacting with many different people. The relationships we have at work help us thrive in our careers—or freefall. That's how important relationships are. The people around you can lighten the load or make things unbearable and difficult. We like to surround ourselves with reliable people we can work well with, but unfortunately, that isn't always possible.

Sometimes, your co-workers, boss, clients, or customers can be difficult to work with and interact with. The more time we spend with these people, the more likely we will be disappointed, upset, or even just annoyed by them. Everyone faces this challenge at some point, but the Bible says it's up to us to live peaceably with everyone.

We don't have to show up for every drama, and we should never blame a clown for acting like a clown; just stop going to the circus. When you understand that God puts you in places for a reason, and if you want to be a person who makes a difference, then be ready for difficult people. Instead of complaining about how chaotic things and other people are, look for a way to be a peacemaker. Maybe you're there to be the person of peace.

Today's scripture instructs us to be aware and attentive, even to our enemies. However, the passage comes with the caveat "as far as it depends on you." Some people will be challenging no matter what you do, and it may be impossible for your relationship with people like this to be completely peaceful. God promised that when you do your part, you'll flourish, while the one being difficult will feel the heat like "coals of fire on his head." All God asks of you is to do your part to promote peace.

Scan here for today's video

"The reason I have given so much is because God has given me so much. We're just trying to be obedient to what God has called us to do."

– David Green
Hobby Lobby

DAY 28:

GOD BLESSES A GENEROUS SPIRIT

"Honor the Lord with your wealth, with the first fruits of all your crops."

Proverbs 3:9, NIV

When you look at everything you have in life, you'll find you've been blessed in various ways. That doesn't mean you haven't seen tough times or challenging circumstances, but it's valuable to step back, see the good in your life, and be grateful. We can and should appreciate all we have, but we also need to remember who has allowed us to enjoy what we have in the first place.

I have observed three common characteristics in every successful person I've known and admired. First, they possess an undeniable sense of mission. Second, they have a generational mindset about their impact. Third, they exhibit a passionate heart of generosity. The men and women who have built companies, portfolios, foundations, and more understand that money can move mountains and solve many problems. They have found ways to leave a lasting mark on the world. Interestingly, none of them became generous only after making their first ten million; they were generous with very little long before they had major influence. Eventually, God blessed them and entrusted them with much more.

There is a gift and blessing of holding onto our gifts with an open hand. After all, what good is wealth if you cling to it with clenched fists?

God calls us to honor Him with our money and the first fruits of our income. But this is just the starting point when it comes to giving; it's like kindergarten. This next part is specifically for my high performers reading this: I want you to come up with a long-term giving goal and pick a percentage. Beyond the kindergarten level, what percentage of giving would you like to achieve?

Anne Frank once said, "No one has ever become poor by giving." God blesses generosity and a giving spirit, and you'll find that when you give back to God and are generous with your resources, you will always have more than enough!

Scan here for today's video

«The more you give, the more you get. Because giving is simply a way of letting more life flow through you.»

– Robert Kiyosaki

DAY 29:

STEP OUT IN FAITH

"In the same way, faith by itself,
if it is not accompanied by
action, is dead."

James 2:17, NIV

What does your faith look like? Chances are, in order to get to where you are now, you had to exercise some level of faith. There are no promises in the world, and everyone has to accept some kind of risk to take that first step toward success. Imagine if you had never taken that step. Where would you be today?

We don't grow at the speed of information but implementation. Everything you have yet to accomplish is on the other side of the unknown. I remember getting on a plane headed to Beijing to meet with some people about a student exchange company I had co-founded. I don't speak Chinese and while I had some marketing materials, I was not an educator or a background in education. We had no clients at all, I was going on the faith that we were able to solve a problem and the Lord had opened an opportunity. I prayed a lot, we worked very hard to get momentum and it worked. We grew that business, started a tour company and a college coaching program. We ended being featured at Colombia University in Master's Program that highlighted our growth and impact we had on kids lives from China and Korea. There were many times I wanted to give up before it started but when you know God's leading you, we must take the leap. Ironically, this devotional is also a journey of faith in action, and I know there's more God wants to do in your life. The bible tells us without faith it's impossible to please God. We can trust an unknown future to a known God.

It's not enough to simply believe in possibilities and have dreams. Having faith is only one part of the equation. Faith without action is ineffective! You can pray, "God, I want to grow this company," and have all the faith in theworld, but if you never develop a strategy, a team or an action plan what good is your faith?

Is there something in your life that you need to accomplish? Trust in God and take action! He wants you to have faith, but He also wants you to take a step—in faith—toward what you are praying for. Put action with your faith and see what God will do!

Scan here for today's video

"Inaction breeds doubt and fear. Action breeds confidence and courage. If you want to conquer fear, do not sit home and think about it. Go out and get busy."

– Dale Carnegie

DAY 30:

ALL FOR GOD'S GLORY

> "So whether you eat or drink or whatever you do, do it all for the glory of God."
>
> 1 Corinthians 10:31, NIV

Your work is important to you—and for good reason. Through your career, you not only support yourself and your family financially, but you also give back to your community in the process. Working well and having a good name is also a way you can bring glory to Christ.

We often consider our primary vocation the biggest way we honor God, but we can easily overlook the little things. Paul tells us that even the menial things we do, the things we may not think of as important, are avenues we can use to glorify God. You may have heard the statement, "How you do anything is how you do everything." We need to conduct ourselves well in everything we do. Everything.

Have you ever met someone who works with a high level of excellence? There are some areas that will be easy for you and others that will take work. I am not talking about perfection, but to be must be mindful and thankful for everything God has given us.

You and I were built for a purpose: by God, for God. Because of this, God calls us to live a life that glorifies Him. There are so many ways we can do this! Honoring our parents and loving our families, respecting those in authority, loving our neighbors as ourselves, being generous with our resources—and the list goes on. Even something as simple as treating your body as the temple—feeding it with nutritious and fresh foods glorifies God. He created you for greatness, and He lives in you. Make sure the way you do even the little things reflects the God-greatness inside of you.

Scan here for today's video

"Don't measure yourself by what you have accomplished, but by what you should have accomplished with your ability."

– John Wooden

DAY 31:

SEEK AND OBEY

"Do not conform to the pattern
of this world but be
transformed by
the renewing of your mind.
Then you will be able to test and
approve what God's will is—His
good, pleasing,
and perfect will."

Romans 12:2, NIV

Chances are, many things you do have been influenced by societal patterns and other people. If the people you surround yourself with have good character, you have probably developed many of their good habits. However, it's sometimes difficult to avoid those engaging in negative behavior, and we may find ourselves slipping into their mistakes. You don't want to miss your opportunity by being in the right place with the wrong mindset. Paul warned us about this pattern in the world and advised us to handle it by having a transformed mindset. Our mind controls the whole body, so we have to keep it healthy, growing, and alert.

Instead, we are called to walk in wisdom and consider things from God's point of view. Daily, we need to renew our minds.

As you go about your day, remember that God has a unique and purposeful plan for your life. Seek His will by renewing your mind with His truth. There won't always be a big sign of what direction you should take, but as long as you seek Him and obey His commandments, your life will work out the way it is meant to.

Scan here for today's video

"The more you trust Jesus and keep your eyes focused on Him, the more life you'll have. Trusting God brings life. Believing brings rest. So stop trying to figure everything out, and let God be God in your life."

– Joyce Meyer

DAY 32:

REJOICE ALWAYS

"Rejoice always, pray continually,
give thanks in all circumstances;
for this is God's will for you in
Christ Jesus."

1 Thessalonians 5:16-18, NIV

Productive, high-achieving, driven people make things happen. They are resourceful, keep their head down, overcome obstacles, and get things done. It is easy to become a bulldozer. Always pushing through, even hard circumstances, but maybe mowing down people around you with little thought to your attitude or what carnage you leave behind you as you go. How do you press onward, advancing the ball and crushing it without crushing everybody around you?

In Paul's letter to the Thessalonians, he gave us a clue. Rejoice always. Pray continually—which just means you keep an open dialogue with God throughout the day; that doesn't mean you sequester yourself in a prayer room somewhere for hours. And give thanks in every circumstance. Never let anything block us from seeing God's goodness—not even our own competence and abilities. Every good thing you have and are capable of is God's gift. This alone gives us reason to express gratitude to our Heavenly Father. It's easy to focus on what's not happening but we have to fight and focus on what is good.

This element of prayer is a very powerful weapon given to all of us that's intended to be used every day. When your prayer is simply talking to God, there aren't a bunch of rules.

God's will for you is to rejoice, pray, and give thanks in all circumstances. By choosing to focus on the good and be grateful for what you have, you can find joy and peace during any situation. This helps you align your life with God's will.

Scan here for today's video

DAY 33:

SPEAK LIFE INTO OTHERS

"Do not let any unwholesome talk come out of your mouths, but only what is helpful for building others up according to their needs, that it may benefit those who listen."

Ephesians 4:29, NIV

You encounter negative circumstances every day. Sooner or later, you will witness the shortcomings of your clients or colleagues, and people will let you down. The way you respond to these situations is what matters. Life and death are in the power of the tongue, which is why what we say is important, even when faced with disappointments.

Unfortunately, gossip and derogatory speech—what Paul calls "unwholesome talk" is extremely easy to fall into. However, God calls us to speak only words that will build others up and benefit the listener. Talking badly about someone behind their back or being rude to someone to their face is not constructive or helpful. Rather, speaking these negative and degrading words can only harm and destroy—not only them but also your reputation.

Consider your words and be intentional in maintaining uplifting, encouraging, and beneficial speech in conversation. You'll be amazed at how attracted people will be to you!

Scan here for today's video

"If you have a positive attitude and constantly strive to give your best effort, eventually you will overcome your immediate problems and find you are ready for greater challenges."

– Pat Riley

DAY 34:

HE STRENGTHENS US

"I can do all this through Him who gives me strength."

Philippians 4:13, NIV

It's true; life is full of obstacles. Leaders face tough decisions daily, need to forecast the future, pivot in the ever-changing present, and answer challenges no amount of preparation can help them avoid. Sometimes, it can be tough to know what to do, and some things are hard to push through, but the Bible says that God will help us deal with whatever we may face. As we navigate life, we need strength to handle the difficulties thrown at us. Today's verse reminds us that God empowers us to do great things. He is strong in our weaknesses, and He is able to help us do things we thought were impossible.

There is a purpose on your life and much for you to do! Too many people go through life with thoughts and dreams that never become a reality. It's not because they don't have a great idea, it's because they don't have the strength to see it through. Remember, you are one person, place or thing away from a major shift forward in your life. God's not asking you figure everything out, but to trust Him. For every trial you will ever face, you have the strength you need.

Whatever challenge you're facing, seek God and trust in His power. He gives you the strength you need to make it through any and every situation. Through Him, you can overcome seemingly insurmountable obstacles. He will cause you to triumph.

Scan here for today's video

"Be sure you put your feet in the right place, then stand firm."

– Abraham Lincoln

DAY 35:

THE STRENGTH OF MY HEART

"My flesh and my heart may fail, but God is the strength of my heart and my portion forever."

Psalm 73:26, NIV

When was the last time your body failed you? Maybe you suffered an injury or are fighting an illness or a disease. When we are wounded or sick, we seek medical treatment. Just as our physical bodies can be ailing, so can our souls.

Troubles aren't just taxing physically and mentally, but sometimes they impact us spiritually as well. This seems to be what the Psalmist had in mind when he wrote today's verse. Sometimes our physical bodies suffer; other times, our spiritual bodies do the same. We are accustomed to treating physical issues because we know the flesh isn't meant for eternity. We are less familiar with treating the pain in our hearts. That pain can only be healed by God.

The good news is that God is faithful. Merciful. Kind. His love for you is greater than you can imagine, and He is always willing to bring life to your ailing soul. God is the strength of your heart and your portion—your source of security, life, peace, and hope—forever.

Scan here for today's video

"As for His failing you, never dream of it — hate the thought of it. The God who has been sufficient until now should be trusted to the end."

– Charles H. Spurgeon

DAY 36:

SEEK THE KINGDOM

*"But seek first His kingdom
and His righteousness,
and all these things will be
given to you as well."*

Matthew 6:33, NIV

What "things" are you pursuing right now? Maybe it's leading your business to a certain level, or it could be reaching a personal goal. These things are good, but while seeking success and achievement, it's easy to get caught up in the desire for status or earthly possessions.

Why is that such a problem? Because even though it is important to be diligent in all our affairs, the more we spend time concentrating on the temporary aspects of why we are here on earth, the further we drift from God's true purpose for our lives. God's plan for you is bigger than your career. Your destiny is bigger than you, and it is certainly bigger than momentary fulfillment.

Today, remember the importance of having an appropriate perspective on life. As you go about your work, focus on God's kingdom and God's righteousness. When you do that, you can trust that He will provide for all your needs— "all these things will be added to you"—and He will bless you in the ways that matter most.

Scan here for today's video

"I realize that a lot of business leaders may disagree with me, but I truly believe that God belongs in what my company does. By putting Him first in my operations, He can bless what I attempt."

– David Green
Hobby Lobby

DAY 37:

ESTABLISH MY STEPS

"In their hearts, humans plan their course, but the Lord establishes their steps."

Proverbs 16:9, NIV

If you aspire to reach certain levels of growth or consistently make a certain income, chances are you have a plan for how you want to get there. While planning is essential to succeeding in any area of life, it's impossible to plot a foolproof path to success.

While planning what steps we want to take, it's easy to forget God is the one who establishes the direction of our lives. The Bible encourages planning and counting the costs, but it also tells us that God is ultimately the one who helps our plans stick. When we faithfully seek God's direction for our lives, He won't let us go down a path that doesn't align with His plan for us. His plans for you are good.

Before venturing too far into your planned course of action, seek God's guidance. Submit your plans to His plans willfully, trusting that He knows what is best for you. When you allow God to establish your steps, you cannot help but go in the right direction.

Scan here for today's video

"I believe God is managing affairs and that He doesn't need any advice from me. With God in charge, I believe everything will work out for the best in the end. So what is there to worry about."

– Henry Ford

DAY 38:

SERVE GOD, NOT MONEY

"No one can serve two masters. Either you will hate the one and love the other, or you will be devoted to the one and despise the other. You cannot serve both God and money."

Matthew 6:24, NIV

Being able to make money is a blessing. After all, you don't work hard in your career to get no reward. There's nothing wrong with earning and accumulating wealth—even vast wealth. The problem comes not from money or earning money but when we develop a **love** of money.

Wealth can go as fast as it was accumulated. It is fleeting, at best. If we try to find our purpose in our work, possessions, and wealth, we will never be happy or fulfilled. As today's verse says, we cannot be dedicated both to God and greedy for more wealth—these cannot go hand in hand! Nothing should be more important to us than following after God. If anything else takes precedence, it hinders our relationship with Him.

The scriptures tell us in Deuteronomy that it's God who gives us the power to gain wealth.

How do you avoid being drawn away from God by the love of money? By making God your priority and seeking to honor Him in all that you do. This way, you can find true meaning and purpose in your work and personal life. Ask yourself, what do you want more, wealth or godliness? If you struggle with loving money or its pursuit, ask God to forgive you and help you make the necessary changes in your life to refocus on the things of God. He'll help you. He loves a heart turned toward His.

Scan here for today's video

"Use money and love people.
Don't use people and love money"

– Joseph Prince

DAY 39:

LOVE GOD AND LOVE OTHERS

"Love the Lord your God with all your heart and with all your soul and with all your mind. This is the first and greatest commandment. And the second is like it: Love your neighbor as yourself."

Matthew 22:37-39, NIV

Loving God with all your heart, especially when we know Him well, can be easy. He is our good Father, our loving Creator, and an ever-present help. But Matthew tells us the second greatest commandment is to love one another. This includes stubborn co-workers, difficult clients, and others we don't naturally get along with.

When it comes to loving our neighbor as we love ourselves, it isn't always easy. People are flawed. Some seek to take advantage of you. Some are just really needy or not very nice, and showing kindness to them can sometimes be difficult. Fortunately, God does not command us to do anything without also equipping us with the tools we need to do it.

Whenever you find it difficult to love others, ask God to give you the patience, gentleness, and kindness you need in interacting with them. Remember, every single person on this planet is a child of God, and when you struggle to love the unlovable, He is faithful to pour His love through you to them. You don't have to do it in your own strength. In fact, you can't. Loving God is the key. Loving people is only possible by God's power at work in you.

Scan here for today's video

"In the business world, treating your customers like friends and your employees like family is what it means to love your neighbor."

– Todd Boffo

DAY 40:

RICH IN REPUTATION

"A good name is more desirable
than great riches;
to be esteemed is better than
silver or gold."

Proverbs 22:1, NIV

You know a person with a good reputation when you see one. Often they are well-respected individuals who others look up to. This is what today's verse is talking about when it mentions "a good name." It's about being admirable, credible, reliable—the kind of person others want to be around.

There is a distinction between striving for a good name and living for the honor of men. One we should do, and the other we should avoid. So, how do we know how to act? The difference is found in what we point others to focus on. We should pray for God's favor and work to grow and be seen so that we can become invisible, allowing others to focus on the One who empowers us.

When I worked for Cardone Industries in Philadelphia (late 90s), they were one of the largest automotive remanufacturers in the world. I remember realizing how big we were as I rode on a golf cart through our distribution center, which was just over a million square feet. I had the privilege of working in the corporate headquarters, and that was something special. We had a corporate saying that was more than a mantra: "We honor God in all we do, We value our work, We value our word, and We value our witness." This is how thousands of employees approached their jobs, our suppliers, our clients, and everyone we encountered on every level. We were known as people who weren't just Christians by words, but by how we lived and worked.

Build a good name for yourself by leaving the print God gave you on this world. When you find your lane for every season of life, you'll be on your way to growing a great name. I cover this topic in my book *PRINTS: Unlocking The Secret For Why You Were Made For More.* The course that goes along with it was designed with you in mind. I will give you a roadmap to understanding your unique and personalized design. When you understand that, you become more confident in the season you're in right now. You aren't guessing or wondering what's missing; you'll have the answers you need to build a legacy.

It's not about being perfect or everyone knowing your name. There's something so incredibly unique about using these godly attributes to live with integrity and honor, building a positive and enduring legacy that will have a lasting impact on those around you. Having a good reputation as someone respectable, honorable, and kind is greater than any wealth you could ever attain.

Scan here for today's video

"Character is like a tree, and reputation is like its shadow. The shadow is what we think of it; the tree is the real thing."

– Abraham Lincoln

NOTES

The 40

NOTES

The 40

NOTES